The Dance In the Kitchen

Jane Sellier

JANE SELLIER

This book is a work of non-fiction. Names of characters, places and incidents are products of both the author's imagination and based on certain historical facts. Any resemblance to actual persons, living or dead, business establishments, events or locales are entirely coincidental.

Copyright 2019 Jane Sellier

All Artwork by the Author

ISBN: 978-1-945190-71-1

FV-6HB

This book, or parts thereof, may not be reproduced without permission. The scanning, uploading and distribution of the book via the Internet or via any other means, including storage in any form of informational or retrieval system without the express written consent of the publisher, except for newspaper, magazine or other reviewer who wish to quote brief passages in connection with a review, is illegal and punishable by law. Your support of Author's rights is encouraged and appreciated.

First Edition: October 2019

www.IntellectPublishing.com

ACKNOWLEDGEMENTS

Special thanks to my husband, Gene Sellier for his technical assistance and his loving support.
Special thanks also to Judy Bishop-Woods for her expert editing abilities.
Thanks also to Charlotte Mackin and Dillie Wammock for combining their artistic talents that produced the last sketch in this book.

JANE SELLIER

CONTENTS

Chapter 1	PADDY PONY	Page 3
Chapter 2	THE HORSETANK	Page 6
Chapter 3	THE WINDMIL	Page 8
Chapter 4	THE WORKHORSES	Page 10
Chapter 5	WORKING IN THE FIELDS	Page 12
Chapter 6	HE FARM KITCHEN	Page 15
Chapter 7	BATH TIME	Page 17
Chapter 8	WASHDAY	Page 19
Chapter 9	THE PIGS	Page 23
Chapter 10	OINKY	Page 25
Chapter 11	THE SCHOOLHOUSE	Page 27
Chapter 12	SPECIAL EVENTS AT SCHOOL	Page 32
Chapter 13	THE WALK HOME FROM SCHOOL	Page 36
Chapter 14	ANIMAL HUSBANDRY	Page 38
Chapter 15	THE GENERAL STORE	Page 44
Chapter 16	THE AUNTS FROM AFAR	Page 48
Chapter 17	LISTENING TO CORN GROW	Page 51
Chapter 18	WINTER FOOD STORAGE	Page 53
Chapter 19	THE BASEMENT	Page 55
Chapter 20	QUIVER CREEK	Page58
Chapter 21	THE TRAIN DEPOT	Page 61
Chapter 22	THRESHING DAY DINNERS	Page 67
Chapter 23	HOSED DOWN	Page 73
Chapter 24	THE SWAMP ROAD	Page 76
Chapter 25	OTHER THINGS TO FEAR	Page 80
Chapter 26	TOY AND SPARKY	Page 84
Chapter 27	HEDGE ROWS	Page 86
Chapter 28	CHURCH ON SUNDAY	Page 89
Chapter 29	HOMEMADE ICE CREAM &WATERMELON	Page 92
Chapter 30	MOM'S SEWING SKILLS	Page 95
Chapter 31	ELECTRICITY AT LAST!	Page 101
Chapter 32	FREEZER, RADIO, REFRIGERATOR	Page 106
Chapter 33	INDOOR PLUMBING	Page 110
AFTER WORD		Page 113

JANE SELLIER

INTRODUCTION

I've never considered myself very lucky but when I think about where I was born, I realize how lucky I've been. Imagine – of all the places I might have been born that I was born in the United States of America! Raised on a farm in central Illinois with 280 acres so I was able to get acquainted with all the good things in the world – hard work, good food, loving parents, pets, alfalfa fields, cornfields, wheat and soybean fields, sand hills, vetch, lespedeza and on and on and on.

Hedge rows and haystacks, haylofts and horses and horse tanks. Pigs and pigpens, chickens and chicken pens and coops. I gathered eggs and sometimes got nipped when the hen wasn't ready to relinquish her deposit. I had an older brother to play ball with and a bicycle which I rode up and down our long, dusty dirt lane. A pig and a pony were my best friends.

In a word, I was blessed.

JANE SELLIER

The Dance In the Kitchen

Jane Sellier

THE DANCE IN THE KITCHEN

CHAPTER 1

PADDY PONY

When I was six years old, my dad gave me a pony. Her name was Paddy. She was a Shetland pony and was russet colored with a white mane and tail. I rode her bareback. Riding bareback is fine except without stirrups to support weight on your feet, you get a pretty good jolting when starting and stopping. Galloping is smoother because of the rhythm established between horse and rider once you get going. Paddy pony and I rode over every square inch of those 280 acres. My pigtails flying out behind me.

Sometimes I'd braid Paddy's mane and tail. We were quite a pair. I groomed her with a curry comb and brush until her mane and tail were all straightened out and shone brightly. And brushed and brushed until her hair was soft and shiny too. She loved it. I loved her, and she knew it because I told her so. I loved that I could hop on her back and we could take off and go just where we wanted. Such freedom!

Often times dad asked me to hop on Paddy and together we'd go out to the pasture and round up the cows and herd them back to the barn. The lane leading to the pasture was on the north side of the barn lot and was overhung with hedge trees – about a quarter mile long. It was a wonderful, private place – cool with dappled shade and lots of birds. Paddy and I would slowly walk through this verdant world. She enjoyed it too because she'd pause occasionally to nibble a leaf or grass.

Paddy knew what to do when we got to the pasture where the cattle were and went around back and forth like a herding dog rounding them up. When all were assembled, we'd amble back down the lane to the barn. The cows would drink at the horse tank and go into the barn where dad forked alfalfa into their troughs and, in general, got them bedded down for the night. I'd curry and brush Paddy too after she'd had her drink and hay.

One day Paddy dumped me head over heels (over her head) into the horse tank.

My brother and I attended a one room country schoolhouse and we both rode Paddy pony to school. I was in the 1st grade and he was in the 8th. He forgot to hold onto her reins one day while opening the barn lot gate and as soon as the gate was open, Paddy made a dash for the horse tank and stopped abruptly in front of it. Inertia being what it is, I flew over her head and landed with a splash in the water – 2 ½-3 ft. deep.

Paddy had a good drink and I had a good soaking.

CHAPTER 2

THE HORSE TANK

Ah-h-h-h-h the horse tank. I had a couple of playmates over one hot, summer day. We played around the house for a long time but when we got all dirty and hot and sweaty, we decided to use the horse tank as a swimming pool. Only one problem – the horse tank contained dad's prize Koi. "Never mind," we said and carefully laid the fish on the ground beside the horse tank until we were done swimming. We had a happy time splashing around and laughing until we were cooled off.

When we put the fish back in the horse tank, we noticed they floated to the top and weren't swimming but we thought they'd be fine, so we didn't say anything about it to anyone. We didn't even consider they might be dead, but we had certain verification of that fact when dad discovered them floating.

I leave what followed his discovery to your imagination. Suffice to say he was very angry!

CHAPTER 3

THE WINDMILL

And, of course, there wouldn't have been any water in the horse tank at all if it hadn't been for the windmill right next to it providing the energy to pump the water out of the ground. Dad had made a loop out of baling wire that fit down over part of the front of the structure so that when the wooden handle lever was secured with it, the blades of the windmill stopped turning and the water stopped flowing. If we forgot to stop it, the horse tank would overflow.

At other times when there was hardly any wind, the windmill was on for hours to try to squeeze a drop or two of water out of the earth and into the tank. Sometimes dad even had to pump by hand to freshen the water in the horse tank for the livestock.

I don't know how tall the windmill was, but it seemed to reach halfway to heaven. There was a ladder built into the metal framework at one corner which I frequently climbed to get to the platform at the top. The platform was a little way under the blades and provided a good vantage point to look around. I could see for miles around in all directions. With the blades stopped, it was a quiet, solitary place to sit and take things in. I was up there often enough so that when mom couldn't locate me around the house, she'd look for me atop the windmill. Don't know how old I was – probably eight of nine.

The barnyard was divided into a cow lot on one side of the horse tank and a horse lot on the other side. The fence separating the two went from the middle of the horse tank to the barn. There was a gate in the middle of the fence between the two lots. Cows were always on one side and horses always on the other side. Each lot was about an acre in size.

CHAPTER 4

THE WORKHORSES

Besides Paddy, we had three big workhorses – Rock, Jack and Buck. Rock was a beautiful, gentle gray speckled Percheron. Jack was reddish brown and not so gentle. Buck was basically brown and so was named because he liked to buck. I was told more than once not to take any chances when around Buck particularly when I was behind him. He also liked to kick with his hind feet. Dad said he liked the fact that all the horses' names ended with the same two letters and that they would respond even if he just made the sound of the first letter in their names.

Rock was a calm hard worker, easy to handle and cooperative. Jack had a skittish streak in him and wasn't very cooperative. He was finer boned than Rock and, compared to Rock, looked more like a racehorse. Rock had long, silky hair on his feet and we kept it clean and combed until it glistened in the sunlight. He seemed to take pride in his appearance and held his head high in a dignified way. He walked with a gait that indicated confidence.

Jack, on the other hand, was proud of himself and held his head high too and walked confidently but with an air of sassiness like a teenager. I couldn't ride him, but I rode Rock. He was so huge that I felt like a mere speck on his back and held the reins firmly in one hand and a handful of his mane in the other. I could stretch out fully on his back and enjoyed doing so, looking up at the sky and feeling the horse underneath. Often I'd lean forward and put my arms around his neck and whisper in his ear that I loved him. His huge eyeball would roll around to try to see me as if to say, "I love you too."

Jack and Buck didn't work well together as a team, so they had to be hitched up with Rock. It was as if Rock told his younger team partners what and how to do things; commands my dad would give them as they provided the energy for what they were pulling. Sometimes a plow or a harrow, or it could be a manure spreader. Once in a while it was a wagon loaded high with hay or corn.

CHAPTER 5

WORKING IN THE FIELDS

In the cool (sometimes bitter cold) fall weather, dad would hitch a team of horses to a big wagon and we'd all go out to the corn fields to shuck corn. We wore old, warm clothes some which were removed as the day and the work progressed. It was hot, sweaty work despite the cool fall weather. We all had a corn picking device (corn shucker) on our right hand that helped separate the ear of corn from the stalk. The corn was ripe, and the stalks were dried and crunchy and there was a snapping, crunching sound when the ear of corn was broken off. As each ear of corn was picked, it was tossed high up into the air and fell in the wagon. The horses ambled along pulling the wagon and stopped from time to time when dad gave them the command.

Often the ground was dry and dusty and, as the horses advanced with the wagon, a plume of dust rose around their feet and into the air. That made for a combination of the smells of fall – the smell of dust and fresh fall air mingled with the scent of the earth and dried leaves that hung on the cornstalks. Quite often it took all day to fill the wagon, but we'd take a lunch break and rest a bit. Mom unpacked the lunch she'd made early that morning in the kitchen. It was something like bologna or ham or egg salad sandwiches, potato chips, homemade applesauce, fruit juice and her wonderful cake or pie to top it all off.

When lunch time rolled around, we were all exhausted and, after resting a bit, went back to the routine established in the morning. The horses took the opportunity to rest too and took little naps while standing on their feet.

After we'd rested and had lunch, we'd resume going up and down the rows of corn until the last stalk had been picked and dad would say "That's the one we've been looking for," referring to the last corn stalk in the last row of the last field that needed picking. It was celebrated with a cup of hot chocolate with marshmallows floating on top when we returned to the house.

The scent and sounds of fall were in the air. Canada geese let us know as they honked their way over our land that it was getting close to winter as they followed their annual migration route to more southern climes. A lot of kernels of corn inevitably dropped to the ground while we were taking it off the stalk and that made a great feeding ground for the migratory geese.

Dad acquired a corn picking machine pulled by a tractor after a while and even more kernels of corn landed on the ground as it went through the field. There were always big flocks of geese grazing on the corn in the stubble fields and, after eating their fill, they would tuck their heads under their wings and sleep.

CHAPTER 6

THE FARM KITCHEN

Ah-h-h, the kitchen! A large, warm place with a wood burning cookstove and no running water. We had no indoor plumbing or electricity until much later. Mom would get up early every morning -winter, summer, spring and fall – and put wood in the big, black cookstove so the burners and oven would be hot enough for her to prepare her meals. She had a degree in Home Economics and was both a super cook and baker. There was a teakettle on one of the back burners steaming away so hot water was always available for tea and other beverages. The water had to be carried in from the pump right outside the back door to the kitchen and it was often my task to pump a bucketful and carry it in.

There were separate buckets filled with water. The buckets of water used for cooking were "cleaner" and were the same ones we used to put milk in. The water we used for bathing was put in just any old bucket. Some of the water was put in the built-in boiler in the stove to keep it hot so it was ready to use for washing dishes or other household chores as well as bathing.

CHAPTER 7

BATH TIME

Bathing was quite an ordeal. A big, round galvanized tub was by the stove in the kitchen and we all bathed in it. I got to go first because I was the youngest, mom went after me and my dad and brother took turns going next depending on who was the cleanest. Of course, the water cooled with each bather, so mom would pour hot water from the teakettle in the tub when I was done so it would be warm for her. She'd also pour hot water in when she was finished so my brother bathed in hot water too. Then my brother would add hot water when he finished so dad's bath would be warm enough.

Bathing in the winter months was less frequent than in the summer but the routine was pretty much the same except that in the hotter months less hot water was used for each bather and everyone took a bath every day. Farming is hard, sweaty work and, remember, we didn't have electricity so there was no air conditioning. Sometimes my dad and brother splashed each other outside with water from the pump before even entering the house to start the cooling off process.

CHAPTER 8

WASHDAY

Every Monday was washday and it took most of the day. The wash house was a yellowish red tile block building about fifty feet from the house. It was a building with two rooms. One was three times larger than the other. The big room had a wood burning cookstove in it but instead of having a built-in water boiler, it had an oval shaped copper boiler on the left side double burners on the top. Early on washday mornings, mom would also build a roaring fire in that stove, so the water would be piping hot when she got all her inside tasks done and could then go out to the wash house to do the laundry.

The laundry consisted of several pairs of dad's dirty denim bib overalls as well as his chambray shirts, socks, undershirts and the rest of the rough and tough clothes he wore in the fields and barn every day. Things like dark blue and bright red bandanas that he wrapped around his head under his straw hat when he worked outside in the summer heat to keep the sweat from running down in his eyes. All his work clothes became extremely dirty and, when he took his clothes off at night, they could almost stand up by themselves. I well remember the scrubbing mom did on the washboard she'd placed in a square galvanized tub – repeating the up and down strokes hundreds of times to remove the soil. I also remember the smells associated with the activity. Hot, soapy water steaming up in one tub with just a hint of bleach smell and the fragrance of homemade lye soap.

Mom made her own lye soap using the fat left over from butchering hogs. She'd pour the lye soap mixture into a shallow, rectangular pan where it remained for several days until it had "set up." Then she'd cut it into bars using a strong, sharp knife. On washday she'd use that same strong, sharp knife to shave off thin pieces of lye soap into the boiling hot water and stir it all up with a wooden handle that had once been the handle of a broom. There's nothing very pretty or sweet smelling about lye soap except maybe the smell of cleanliness and it certainly did get a lot of the dirt out of the clothes.

Washing the overalls came last in the lineup of clothes to be washed. The white shirt dad wore to church, our undies and other light-colored clothes were laundered first. Those clothing items were the first to be plunged in the clean, steaming hot soapy water. Mom added a bit of bleach to this water and everything came out sparkling clean. There were two other square tubs nearby as well filled with clear, clean water. These were the rinse tubs. The light-colored clothes were first in these tubs, followed by increasingly darker colored garments. Often the clothes needed a second rinsing and the water in the first rinse tubs was drained out into five-gallon buckets so it could be put on the garden plants later. Sometimes the first rinse water was too soapy to be put on plants, so it was just dumped out back of the building. The second rinse water could almost always be put on the plants – or in the pig slop.

The yard around the house had a white picket fence around it and dad and my brother had built several long clotheslines inside. After washing and rinsing the laundry, everything had to be hung on the clotheslines to dry. I enjoyed hanging up the clothes because they smelled fresh and wooden clothespins were used to secure them to the aluminum clothesline. It was necessary to wipe over all the clotheslines to remove the dirt before hanging up the clean things.

Some days were sunny and breezy so immediately after being secured to the line, the clothes started flapping in the breeze. Other days when rain threatened, the clothes just hung there limply and all we could do was hope the sun would come out. On days when the sun didn't appear and, as evening approached, we'd have to take the clothes down and try to find enough places to hang them either on the screened-in porch by the kitchen or string up makeshift clotheslines in the house. Eventually, they were dry and could be folded or hung and put away, but it was different in the winter.

The clothes washing procedure was pretty much the same summer and winter except that in the winter the clean clothes often froze on the clothesline. Very often we trudged through snow just to get to the clotheslines and our fingers nearly froze while hanging the clean clothes up. We only hung clothes out in the winter if the sun was brightly out but, even then, they'd freeze and taking them down at the end of the day was quite a chore. Everything was stiff as a board and it was quite an effort not only to get them inside but also to find enough space for them to hang, thaw out and dry.

It often took days to complete the weekly laundry – especially in the winter.

CHAPTER 9

THE PIGS

The pigs lived in a pig house built a little distance from the barn. It was a separate pole building at one side of the pig pen closed in on three sides with an open front and slant roof. There was no floor, but dad always kept it clean by pitching mounds of clean, golden wheat straw on the ground. The pigs would root around in the straw to bed down or eliminate. The straw was changed as the manure from the pigs made it necessary, but that manure was forked into the manure spreader hitched up to a team of horses and spread as fertilizer on the fields where it was needed

I often rode with dad on the manure spreader as the horses pulled it up and down while the manure was being slung out on the fields behind by rotating iron prongs. The smell was not at all unpleasant as one might imagine. Rather it was an earthy, rich almost spring-like odor. We had a feeling of satisfaction knowing that we were using the pigs' waste to make our soil richer, so we'd have better crops.

The pigs were fed in a long, low wooden trough at right angles to the pig house. Cracked corn and something called "mash" was dumped in the trough from an elevated walkway parallel to the trough. The pigs ate lots of other kinds of things too including slop. Slop was made up of whatever was available from whatever source. This consisted of kitchen scraps such as potato peelings, milk, laundry rinse water, left-overs, plate scrapings – that kind of thing. They ate with gusto and thrived on what we fed them.

There are many different varieties of pigs. We had a variety of Poland Chinas and "Black Belts." We called them "Black Belt" pigs because while they were pinkish-white like the Poland Chinas, they had a wide black stripe all the way around their middle right behind their front legs.

CHAPTER 10
OINKY

Mother pigs are rather clumsy and are not the most attentive to their newly born litter. I came home from school one day to find the cutest, little pink pig that dad had taken from the rest of the litter because the clumsy mother pig had accidentally plunked down on its hind legs and it had difficulty walking. It was love at first sight for me and I named him Oinky. I fed Oinky with a baby bottle filled with warm cow's milk, washed him with soapy, warm water and cleaned and polished his little hooves so they shone.

Oinky knew what time I'd be home from school and anticipated our daily reunion as much as I did. As Oinky grew we became fast friends. His condition improved and I'd take him for walks around the yard helping him when he needed it. He followed me much like a well-behaved dog would and it became part of my daily routine to spend time with him.

One day I said, "Listen, Oinky, and I'll tell you a story" and I told him the story of the three little pigs. You know, the story about the three young pigs who each built a house – one with straw, one with sticks and one with bricks? He loved the story and seemed pleased that there were at least three pigs in the world who had a story written about them and became famous. Maybe it gave him hope for his future. It was hard to tell because Oinky always had a smile on his snout. He was a happy little fellow.

Oinky wasn't there waiting for me one day when I came home from school. I went in the kitchen and asked mom "Where's Oinky?" and she said I'd have to ask my dad. Dad was out in a field plowing but I ran to meet him when I saw him coming back to the barn and asked him, "Where's Oinky?"

He told me that Oinky had gotten too big to keep as a pet and that he'd butchered him that morning. He didn't say it in an unkindly way and tried to make me understand even while sympathizing with me. Of course, I didn't understand and declared that I hated my dad as I bawled my way back to the house.

I still get tears in my eyes when I remember it!

THE DANCE IN THE KITCHEN

CHAPTER 11

THE SCHOOLHOUSE

I attended school at a one room schoolhouse. It was on the corner of two dirt roads near Topeka, Illinois in Mason County. One of the roads was called "Tightrow" although I don't know why. My uncle Pat who was a dentist, gave me a box of stationary once with "The Belle of Tightrow" imprinted at the top of each sheet of paper and on the matching envelopes. I was so proud to have it and eventually used it all up. But I digress.

The schoolhouse was originally a white clapboard building, but it hadn't been painted in years and years so when I went there it was dingy gray with the formerly white paint chipping off in big chunks. It was just a big box shape with four windows along each side. It had a single door at the front below the belfry. The bronze bell in the belfry had a sonorous clang and when it was time for us to come inside again after recess, the teacher would gently and slowly pull the rope attached to the bell, so we heard a soft, rather pleasant tone.

A concrete step by the door kept some of the mud or snow out on inclement days. We took turns sweeping it off. Two cloakrooms were on the left and right when you got inside – one for girls and one for boys. Each had coat hooks along the walls with shelves above where you could hang your coat and put your lunch box and other stuff to be stored until the end of the school day. If our coats got wet while playing outside in the snow, we slung them over empty desks near the coal burning furnace in front of the building to dry. I can still see the steam rising off them as they dried.

Sometimes we'd sit on a long bench near the furnace and have our lessons when we came in from the cold. I remember propping my feet up on an iron railing in front of the furnace and reading my books. There were never more than five or six of us in the whole school although it was for grades one through eight. My brother was in eighth grade the year I was in first and that's the only year I remember an eighth grader being in the school. The building was about 500 square feet and sat on a lot of about 1 ½ acres.

Two outhouses (one for girls, the other for boys) were on the back of the property next to a hedge row that separated the school property from a farmer's field. Trudging out there in inclement weather was no walk in the park especially on rainy or snowy days! Like the schoolhouse, both outhouses had been there a long time and smelled to high heaven. I detest any kind of outdoor facility to this day!

There was a stage at the front of the room with blackboards behind. The teacher's desk sat in the center of the stage. There were maps that were rolled up above the blackboards but could be pulled down if the teacher needed to show us a place on the map. There were also pictures of both George Washington and Abraham Lincoln in plain sight on the wall behind the stage. An American flag hung to the right of the long blackboard and we said the Pledge of Allegiance every morning.

Our lessons started right after saying the Pledge of Allegiance and the teacher would call one grade at a time up to her desk where we would go over our lessons with her. She went over our homework with us, we'd read a bit or be told about homework pertaining to the next day before returning to our own desks. While one grade was with the teacher, the other grades were at their desks studying. I was usually prepared and did well in my subjects. I particularly liked Reading and Spelling. I loved diagramming sentences and writing stories. I also liked the Geometry side of Arithmetic.

I liked recess too. Once out on the playground, we picked teams (albeit small ones) and each team covered one side of the schoolhouse. The game was called Handy Over, and we'd try to throw a ball over the building to the other side. I don't exactly remember the object of the game, but I think the opposite team tried to catch the ball then run to the other side and try to tag someone. If tagged, that person had to join the other team. This went on until all the members of one team were tagged and on the other team -or- until the teacher rang her little hand bell to let us know it was time to come inside where the lessons continued until it was time to go home for the day.

In the winter, snow accumulates and is blown by the wind into fantastic shapes making everything look shiny clean and beautiful but mysterious. Ordinarily dull looking fences are transformed into shapes that would be impossible for any artist to recreate. My brother and I still rode Paddy pony to school through the deep snow on these cold winter days. Dad had built a small shed on the school grounds for Paddy to stay in during the day, so she had a dry place to rest until we rode her back home at the end of the school day. There was also a trough in Paddy's shed with hay and, of course, water for her to drink.

It was my brother's and my responsibility to clean her droppings out of the shed, add clean straw to the floor and make sure she always had hay to eat and clean water to drink. At the end of the school day, we'd hop on Paddy's back, close the shed, and she'd get us safely home again. Paddy had to be brushed and put in her stall in the barn where we provided her with fresh hay and water before we plodded through the snow to the house.

Hot chocolate and home-made cookies were always ready for us at the end of the school day and mom, my brother and I would talk about "our day." After enjoying this treat, I sat at the kitchen table and started my homework. As daylight waned, the kerosene lamp on the table was lit and I often finished my homework by lamplight while mom was preparing supper. The smells coming from her endeavors on the stove were tantalizing and, when dad and my brother came in from doing evening chores in the barn and outside, we'd all sit down at the big kitchen table and enjoy our supper. Most farmers then called the evening meal "supper" and "dinner" was the mid-day meal.

CHAPTER 12

SPECIAL EVENTS AT SCHOOL

There were two very special events held during the school year and I liked them both. One was a "Box Supper" and the other was the annual Christmas program. The Box Supper was held in the late spring and everyone's parents, grandparents and neighbors were invited to attend. Every student at the school would decorate a cardboard box trying to make it more beautiful than anyone else's box. I spent hours choosing just the right materials (usually crepe paper and ribbon) and carefully cutting and pasting my designs onto my cardboard box. My box was arrayed with the colors of the American flag - bright reds, blues and whites. I remember placing a trio of tiny American flags atop one of my boxes.

I remember embellishing my box with the softer, pastel colors of spring and, if the spring wildflowers were blooming, I'd carefully place a bouquet of fresh flowers that I'd cut on the top of the box. They were held together with a rubber band or a piece of string and placed in a tiny water container hidden from view by fresh foliage.

When everyone had gathered inside the schoolhouse for the Box Supper event, the teacher would stand at her desk on the stage and ask for everyone's attention. She welcomed everyone and made a few announcements and then told everyone about the Box Supper. It was a fundraiser for much needed supplies for the school but, more than that it was a social event. Only the parents knew whose box was whose and, as the bidding started, the excitement grew. Of course, the parents bid (and over bid) on their child's box but grandparents and neighbors and friends didn't know who had decorated each box, so they bid primarily on the way a box looked.

The highest bidder of each box became the recipient and then discovered who had decorated it. The new owner of the box invited the maker of the box to join him/her in eating the delicious food inside. All the boxes were beautifully decorated and the food on the inside contained all items made fresh in other wood burning stove kitchens such things as fried chicken, potato salad, deviled eggs, applesauce, fresh spring lettuce, carrot and celery sticks, fresh apple pie or pudding.

I always put both apple pie and chocolate pudding in my box because I wanted the person who bought my box to have a choice. I always hoped the recipient of my box would ask me which I preferred so I could say, "I like chocolate pudding best. Thanks." Mostly, when the food had been enjoyed, the person who paid for the box would offer it to the maker. I was glad about that and always put the newest box on display with the others in my room.

As Christmas approached each year, and when we had our studies done, we cut red, white and green construction paper in strips and formed them into circles looped and held together with glue. These were strung up in loop-d-loop chains on top of each window and door. They were hung around the pictures of George Washington and Abraham Lincoln too, but we were always careful not to cover their faces. They were draped over the top of the blackboard and on the back of the teacher's desk. The only place we could not hang these brightly colored paper loops was near the wood burning stove.

After lunch the day before the Christmas program, we collected greenery from outside around the schoolyard to add to the paper decorations. There was evergreen, holly with red berries and other vegetation that, when bound together and added to the red, green and white paper loops looked very festive. It smelled good too. We were highly complimented for our efforts by the attendees of the event and it put everyone in a happy, friendly mood.

The rehearsed program was preceded by a potluck dinner. Everyone who came brought something to eat or drink to share. Since it was a Christmas celebration, folks brought cookies of all kinds. There were Marzipan, chocolate chip, Snickerdoodles and Spritz cookies. Some people brought fried chicken, others brought sandwiches or casseroles. The whole affair was quite festive, and everyone had a happy time.

There was a play at Christmas and every student had a part. One year I was Mary, the mother of Jesus, another time I was a shepherd and, finally, a donkey. I was never chosen to be an angel which was what I considered to be the best role. Angels got to wear the prettiest costumes. All white and sparkly and, besides that, they got to hold long, shiny wands! The same year I was a shepherd disguised in a long, drab grayish brown bathrobe type garment all I got to hold was a crooked, ugly brown pole that was a branch chopped off a scraggly tree. The angels waved their sparkly wands around but the pole I held as a shepherd was always supposed to be in touch with the ground and was not supposed to move unless I moved.

During rehearsals, I soon discovered that shepherds don't move much except forward a little to better see the baby Jesus in the manger. Mary, Joseph, the kings and wisemen were all hovering around center stage and the shepherds were kept in the background. The angels were most noticed because of their bright, shiny costumes and because they fanned their wands around to get attention.

CHAPTER 13

THE WALK HOME FROM SCHOOL

If the weather was nice, I'd walk home on the dirt road that lead to the back of our farm and then walk along the fencerow to the barn lot to our house. It wasn't a long walk (maybe a mile). Sometimes I wished it was longer because a boy who lived on a farm near ours walked with me and I had a crush on him. He was tall, dark and handsome. I was tall, scrawny and in pigtails. I'm sure he was glad that the lane leading to his house was closer than the lane leading to my house, so he didn't have to spend more time with me.

I remember crawling through fence rails and climbing over some. Each fenced area had its own gate so the livestock wouldn't get out and each gate had a wooden "slider" as well as a wire loop that fit over a post. The slider had to be replaced and the wire loop had to be repositioned over the post so it was left secure again and none of the livestock could get out.

CHAPTER 14

ANIMAL HUSBANDRY

Occasionally, livestock would "get out" and an all-points bulletin went out. Everyone on the farm where the animal (or animals) resided would stop what they were doing and search for the escapees. If they weren't discovered quickly and brought back to where they belonged, mom would telephone the neighbors asking them to watch for whatever was missing. I remember a couple of times when cows were missing for two days. Everyone was greatly relieved when they were found and that all was back to normal.

Once, after missing for a couple of days, a cow that was finally back in the barn became very bloated. Dad said it was because she ate something that she shouldn't have. She bloated up like a big balloon with both sides sticking way out. Poor thing was in a great deal of pain, but dad acted quickly to relieve her. He took a rather long, sharp knife and, finding just the right spot plunged it decisively into her side. I remember hearing a hissing sound – kind of like air being released from a balloon. He cleaned the wound and the cow felt relief almost immediately. When it was feeding time for cows that evening, she joined the other cows chowing down as if nothing had happened. All farmers had skills like that and were able to treat their livestock quite well. I'm sure lots of animal's lives were saved by that quick, skilled action.

Another time I saw my dad helping a pregnant cow deliver her calf. I hadn't intended to see it and my dad certainly didn't intend me to see it, but I was playing nearby outside and kept hearing bellowing sounds coming from inside the barn. Of course, I had to find out what all the ruckus was about. When I went down the long hallway in the center of the barn, I found my dad and my brother with a cow in the last stall on the left. I was shocked by what I saw! Dad was at the tail end of the cow and had inserted his right arm almost up to the elbow in the birth canal of the cow. My brother was holding the cow's tail out of the way so dad wouldn't get whipped by it. I was mesmerized and continued to watch as the birthing continued. The poor cow continued to bellow and kept turning her head around and strained to look at my dad as if to tell him to quit what he was doing. Of course, she thought it was his fault. Her eyes rolled around in their sockets and she was clearly very stressed.

Finally, though, dad excitedly said, "I've got my hands on its front feet. Hand me that rope over there so I can tie the feet together!" Dad continued to pull, the cow continued to push and soon enough the calves' front feet were visible. My brother handed him the rope and dad tied the legs together. The cow kept pushing and dad kept pulling but now he had to somehow maneuver the calves' head in the proper position so it could exit the birth canal.

The cow seemed to realize that dad was helping her, and she kept pushing. Dad knew just when to assist her and kept pulling. Now they were working as a team and before I knew it, out popped the newborn calf. Dad was there to catch it and lay it gently on the straw on the floor of the stall. My brother immediately assisted by cutting the umbilical cord and everyone heaved a sigh of relief – dad, brother and cow and me. Dad cleaned the cow as best he could with warm, water and the new mother cow set about carefully cleaning her newborn calf with her tongue.

I couldn't swear to it but I'm pretty sure I saw tears in my dad's eyes.

I, of course, immediately had many questions regarding what I had just witnessed like "Why did you have your arm in the back of the cow, What's a breach birth, why did you have to tie a rope around the calves' legs, can I have the calf for a pet?"

Dad was ready for a rest so when he was sure the mother cow and calf were settled, we all went to the house where we told mom about what just happened. She was very happy to hear about the successful delivery – all farmers are happy about new arrivals in their animal population. It increases the size of the herd and, if all goes well, increases the dollars in their checkbooks because it also increases the milk production.

A lot of farmers in our area had electric milking machines but even after our part of the county was connected to electricity, dad continued to milk our cows by hand. I think it was because he'd always done it that way plus we didn't have as many cows to milk as some of our neighbors. He never said so, but I also think it was because he liked squirting the warm cow's milk onto the cats' faces as they gathered around him sitting on his milking stool.

We had lots of cats and most of their faces were white and wet after dad's milking sessions. They spent the next 15 minutes licking and cleaning themselves and, when all cleaned up again, cuddled up together and took long naps.

Something that always amazed and worried me a little was that the kittens had nests in the cows' mangers. I was afraid that the cows would eat them until dad told me that cows are not carnivores. I wanted to know what that meant so it was a "teaching moment" for mom and dad.

"Carnivores are animals that eat other animals," they said.

I was pretty much horrified at that until they reminded me that humans are animals too and that we eat other animals.

"Think of the bacon, steaks and chicken I fix in the kitchen," mom said.

My "yes – buts" and other questions were of no avail and I sure didn't want to stop eating mom's delicious fried chicken, so I kept quiet about carnivorous behavior after that. For some time though I thought about animals eating other animals at most of our meals. I got over it soon enough though and continued to eat fried chicken, bacon, pork chops, steaks, hamburgers, etc. All these "other animals" were raised on our farm and, even though I didn't like the butchering times, I did really like how it all tasted.

There was a chicken house not far from the house where about 150 chickens resided. We'd go to a nearby town in the spring of the year and purchase lots of little, fluffy, yellow adorable baby chicks from a hatchery that specialized in all things chicken, horse, sheep. The store had chicken coops, chicken waterers, chicken food, medicine for chickens – you get the idea.

The baby chicks were loaded up into cardboard boxes that had lots of holes punched in the sides for ventilation. They stacked up one on top of the other and, after we'd loaded them into the car, away we went. It was ten miles from the town to our farm and all the way home we heard the high-pitched chirping of the baby chicks.

We'd spent several days before the purchase of the new baby chicks carefully cleaning out the chicken house. All the old ground up corn cobs that had been on the floor for the last batch of chickens was removed. The wooden floor was swept and, finally, we used lye water to scrub the floor. It was left to dry for several days before we put clean ground up corn cobs on the floor for the new crop of chickens so when we arrived home with them, the chicken house was shiny clean and ready to welcome them to their new home. All the waterers and food containers had also been cleaned so there was no fear of disease.

When unloaded, the baby chicks scampered around their new environs glad to be out of the confining cardboard boxes. I can still hear them cheeping. Mom made the comment that "That's a lot of future fried chicken!" and I remember not caring very much for that remark.

Chickens are messy to deal with. They scratch their food out of their food containers, spill waterers, poop all over the place (even in their food and water) and peck at each other. Sometimes they must be separated because they pick and peck so much on each other. It may be territorial, but I always thought it was more like bullying.

Maybe it's the survival of the fittest. I don't know but it's not a pretty sight.

CHAPTER 15

THE GENERAL STORE

There was a small village about three miles from our farm. My uncle and aunt owned and operated the general store there. My uncle was also the postmaster which required him to place the letters that came to his post office each day in various cubby holes. The mail was delivered to him daily by train in a big canvas bag that had been tightly tied at the top. He'd meet the train, pick up the bag and walk back to the post office.

The recipients of the letters could pick them up after a certain time. I think it was 2 o'clock. Since no keys were issued to the box holder, my uncle had to get the contents of the boxes for the recipient each time they asked for their mail. The boxes were behind a very small service window in the very small post office with a little counter where people could rest their elbows until my uncle returned with their mail. The window was covered with metal bars, so the mail had to be shoved underneath the bottom rail. It looked like many banks used to look. I think the idea was not to let the customers have easy access to what lay beyond the wall and little window with bars. There was never a robbery that I remember so I guess it worked.

The general store was a huge, two story white clapboard building with two steps leading to the double front door. Big bay windows were on both sides of the front door where my aunt and uncle could display some of the wares they offered for sale. There were hundreds of things inside and only room for a small percentage of those things in the windows, but it let people know what the latest products were.

Upon entering the building, you were confronted with a long aisle all the way to the back of the building and on each side of the aisle were tables containing all kinds of things. There were bib overalls, men and women's underwear, shoes, cotton and woolen socks, leather and twine shoestrings, bandanas, sun hats, winter scarves, hats, mittens and gloves. There were also wash tubs, hoses, rakes, shovels, garden tools, watering cans as well as bolts of cloth and lace.

Many women had good sewing skills in those days and made everything from clothes for themselves and their families to curtains, drapes, bedspreads, pillow covers, etc. for their homes. There wasn't room for everything to be displayed so there were boxes filled with things way up on the topmost shelf that was accessed by a sliding library ladder. If you wanted or needed an item that you didn't see and asked, my aunt would slide the ladder over and position it below the box that held it and bring it down for inspection. The inventory was enormous, and they could provide almost everything their customers needed or wanted.

I was one customer who particularly liked their ice cream freezer. It was way in the back of the store. When I entered the store in the summer months, my uncle or aunt would ask me if I'd like an ice cream cone. Silly question! There was vanilla, strawberry and chocolate ice cream so I'd have a different flavor with each visit.

The huge second story room of the general store was accessed by a long stairway on the outside of the building. The community held meetings there occasionally and my mom and dad usually attended. Of course, I'd go too, and it was a great opportunity to play with other children in the area. There were many trees and wood piles out back on the property and we'd play Hide and Seek until it was time to go home.

The general store was open one night each week and dad would join other farmers in the area for a "night out" playing cards. In the summer, the electric overhead fans made the heat tolerable and, in the winter, the pot-bellied stove kept the men warm as they played cards. I went with my dad once in a while if mom had plans to be away from home too.

Sometimes she had a rehearsal for an event scheduled at our church. Once she was in a kitchen band and "played" the pans. Other times she accompanied the rest of the band on the piano.

CHAPTER 16

THE AUNTS FROM AFAR

I had two aunts that were very special to me. They were my mother's sisters. One lived in a big city in northern Illinois and the other lived in a medium sized town in central Illinois. My Aunt Evangeline. would take a train from the city where she lived to the small town where my Aunt Mary lived and stay there until it was time to go back after Christmas. We always hoped that they would be able to join us for our family Christmas celebration.

Sometimes the snow was so deep we feared the roads would be impassable. There were many dirt roads between our houses – a distance of about thirty miles. Aunt Mary had a 1949 Ford sedan and was a good driver, so they never failed to make the trip. I liked my aunts but, as a youngster, what I liked even more were all the presents they brought. Clothes, books, dolls, toys which were all wrapped in pretty paper. They were "townies" and wore fancier clothes than we did so it was always interesting to see them in, what seemed to me, their elegant attire.

Mom always prepared a sumptuous Christmas feast – ham, turkey, wild duck or goose that dad and my brother had shot in the stubble-field early that very morning. The meat was served with all the trimmings – mashed potatoes and gravy, sweet potatoes, cranberry sauce, two or three vegetables, Jell-O salads and PIES! Chocolate, coconut cream, apple and pumpkin. All was prepared to perfection on the top or in the oven of the wood burning kitchen stove.

I was not able to participate only one year. I had the mumps and had to stay on the daybed in the dining room and was able to just listen and watch. After everyone had eaten, they sat and visited for a while, then the chairs were pushed back, and we all adjourned to the living room. My immediate family had decorated the Christmas tree a few days before and, when everyone was gathered in the living room, dad lit the candles that were firmly attached to the branches. The soft light from the candles made the ornaments on the tree sparkle.

When we finally got electricity a couple years later, we did the same routine except dad said, "OK, everyone, come in the living room. I have a surprise for you." All dad had to do then was plug in the cord to the big, colored bulbs we'd attached to the tree branches, stand back and listen to us all "oohing" and "aahing." The gifts were retrieved from under the Christmas tree and distributed and unwrapped. It was a happy time, and everyone truly liked the gifts they received.

My mom played Christmas carols on the piano in the living room and we all gathered around and sang. The words to the songs were familiar because we sang them at home, in school and in church – Silent Night, Oh Come All Ye Faithful, We Three Kings of Orient Are, Joy to the World. Jingle Bells, Rudolph the Red Nosed Reindeer and White Christmas were also sung and, with each tune sung, our voices got louder and louder until we were laughing so much we had to sit down.

Mom went to the kitchen to make fresh coffee and offered a second piece of pie. Aunts Evangeline and Mary would say things like "I'm still full of dinner" or "Oh, I don't think I could eat another bite" but, of course, when the smell of fresh coffee hit their nostrils, they changed their minds. They usually left fairly early to drive back to Aunt Mary's house so they could get back right before dark. It was an old-fashioned Christmas to be sure but I can still see them in their dress up clothes, fur coats and galoshes. They were two nice ladies.

I remember one time when I sent thank you notes to them both, I added "My birthday is May 5th." I suppose I figured it couldn't hurt to remind them.

CHAPTER 17

LISTENING TO CORN GROW

Did you know that if you listen carefully, you can hear corn growing? It's true! There was a cornfield close to the house and on hot, summer evenings after supper, I liked to go outside and lay down between the rows and listen to all the sounds. The sounds were different depending on the time of evening. If the sun was just setting, the insects were still buzzing around and had to be swatted away. If it was dusk, the birds were hurrying to their places of rest for the night. I particularly enjoyed laying on my back about mid-field. The air was still very warm, but the earth was cool. It didn't matter how dirty I got because I'd have my bath when I went back to the house.

While laying quietly between rows of corn, I heard a myriad of sounds – the flapping of birds' wings, birds chirping, insects buzzing and the subtle popping of corn growing as it sought its way upward towards the sky. It's a sound that soothes the soul and I frequently fell asleep and didn't wake up until I heard mom calling my name from the porch on the side of the house. It was all very relaxing, and, after my bath, I was ready for bed.

CHAPTER 18

WINTER FOOD STORAGE

The squirrels scratched in the colorful, crispy fallen leaves harvesting nuts and putting them in their larders so they would have food throughout the cold, snowy winter. Like the geese and squirrels, we also put food aside to be enjoyed in the winter. We had several apple trees of different kinds. Some were red, some yellow and it was my task to put as many as I could in a bushel basket and haul them up to the kitchen in my Radio Flyer wagon. The wagon had slats made of wood on the sides and often I'd also put apples around the sides of the basket in the bottom of the wagon.

Mom and I carefully peeled and cored each apple and placed the slices in a pan with a little water. It was "apple sauce making day" and while she proceeded with the other steps necessary, I would return with the now empty bushel basket to the apple orchard and pick more apples. This continued until we finally had enough apples simmering on the stove to make many quarts of sauce. The sauce was then sealed in glass canning jars and stored in the larder in the basement.

You can imagine how good it tasted when the snowdrifts outside in the cold winter were two or three feet high. It was like eating a mouthful of summer. Each winter mom said, "We'll can more applesauce next fall" but when the time rolled around again, we quickly tired of peeling all those apples so we usually ended up with the usual three dozen quarts.

CHAPTER 19

THE BASEMENT

The basement under the house had a dirt floor, was dark and dingy but good things took place there. The furnace was huge with aluminum ducts running to various registers placed in the floor of upper rooms. There was no blower on the furnace to direct the heat from the furnace upward and, as heat naturally rises, we relied on that to warm the upstairs. The main floor was comfortably warm most of the time but, as the house had two stories, the bedrooms on the second floor were chilly.

Occasionally the bedrooms were downright cold, and we slept on feather beds with a pile of blankets on top of us. In summer, it was just the opposite. The bedrooms were hot, and the first floor was a bit cooler – but only by a couple of degrees. No electricity, no fans, no air-conditioning. Even with all the doors and windows open on a breezy day, it was still very hot inside the house. We burned coal in our furnace and there was a big pile of it near the furnace. The coal was delivered every couple of months by truck and the driver scooped it in our coal chute into the basement. It took hours for the coal dust to settle on the dirt floor and everything else that was stored in the furnace room. If mom had too many canned goods to store in the larder, there were additional shelves in a corner of the furnace room where some things were stored. The shelves were covered with a big piece of oil cloth so very little coal dust settled on the jars containing food.

The larder where the canned fruits and vegetables were stored was another room in the basement. It was literally a step up from the furnace room and we considered it the "clean" room. It had a concrete floor and the door between the two rooms kept most of the coal dust out. We also cleaned that room from time to time which was something we almost never did in the furnace room. The clean room had a hole that was six feet deep dug in one corner and, being deeper than the main part of the floor, was much cooler. That hole in the ground served us well as a "refrigerator" and we stored butter, cottage cheese, milk and cream there for table use. Of course, those items had to either be consumed by us at our daily meals or discarded and replaced. Butter and cottage cheese lasted longer but the other milk items were more quickly perishable.

The basement was also accessible through a big horizontal door that was part of the porch floor off the kitchen but, when raised up, revealed stairs that would lead to the clean room below. Mom would often ask me to get her something she needed from the cool hole in the ground when she was cooking or baking. "Go down to the basement and bring up a quart of milk" or "Should we have cottage cheese tonight with our supper?" Mom's home-made cottage cheese was a favorite of mine because she and my dad allowed me to sprinkle sugar on it. There were a few food items that I wasn't particularly fond of, so my parents suggested trying them with a little sugar sprinkled on top. I didn't much care for tomatoes either until they suggested the sugar solution.

CHAPTER 20

QUIVER CREEK

There was another way to cool off in the heat of the summer and that was in Quiver Creek. It was a modest but acceptable flow of water between two sand banks about three miles from the house. I was outside most of the time when I was a child and meandering along the dirt roads to the creek was something I did frequently. I always took my shortcut through the horse lot by the barn and down a long row of hedge trees on the other side. The hedge trees were tall and formed a shaded archway along the dusty dirt path that the horses pulling wagons and other farm equipment often walked up and down.

The path was two wagon wheels wide and had tufts of grass between. The lane ended at a 40-acre field which I crossed near the fencerow and continued until I got to the dirt road that lead to the village where my aunt and uncle's store was. I walked through the village to another dirt road and finally came to the old, rusty steel bridge that crossed Quiver Creek. Quite often I'd meet my friends there – the same friends who went for a swim with me in dad's horse tank!

We thought Quiver Creek was an enchanted place and loved playing there. If we walked a little way along the overgrown banks of the creek, it widened and there was an island in the middle with water flowing lazily around it. The island itself was covered with trees both large and small. Some of the dead trees and branches had fallen and stayed in situ. That only added to the enchantment of the place. It was the perfect spot to build forts and pretend we were pirates or pioneers. We didn't realize at the time that water moccasin snakes considered the creek a great place too but, fortunately, we never encountered one. All we saw swimming in the water were different sizes and kinds of fish.

We also swam in the water. "Swim" is an exaggeration, but we plopped and splashed around in the water to our hearts content. We played there for hours and had a jolly, happy time. We stopped by my aunt and uncle's store on our way home and were all gifted with an ice cream cone; flavor of our choice. "Would you like vanilla, strawberry or chocolate?" my uncle would ask each time.

One time when I was there by myself, he said, "I'm now offering customers ice cream sundaes. How would you like a chocolate sundae?"

I said, "Yes and thank you very much!" I noticed he never made the same offer when my friends were with me, so I felt very special!

After enjoying our ice cream, my friends and I retraced our steps back to our respective homes. They lived in the village so didn't have to walk very far. I followed nearly the same dusty roads and lanes back home but occasionally as I was walking through the yard of a local schoolteacher, she'd spot me and invite me in for lemonade. She and her husband had a large yard and orchard which were beautiful. They were both retired and they both loved gardening and I always marveled at how many kinds of fruit trees, bushes, and ornamental trees they had. Their entire area was ablaze with flowers of many colors and heights and there was not a weed in sight. White picket fences with ornamental gates surrounded some of the flower beds and orchards and their house had a fairy tale look about it.

"I've just made a fresh pitcher of lemonade," she'd say, "Would you like some?"

Her house was far enough away from the general store that, by the time I got there, lemonade sounded great. She always had interesting things to talk about and asked a lot of "teacher type" questions but I liked her and thought of her as a friend. Her name was Elsie. Elmer was her husband. They had no children of their own which might be a reason she rather doted on me. I'm glad I knew them. I considered days like that very special and loved the freedom to walk anywhere I chose; stop anywhere I pleased and spend time with friends and neighbors.

CHAPTER 21

THE TRAIN DEPOT

Going to the depot to meet the train was an everyday occurrence for my uncle. It was his responsibility as postmaster to pick up the canvas bag each day that contained the mail of his many post office customers. Every so often there were packages that had been sent to his customers too and frequently the packages were so large that he had to put them on a big flat bottom wagon and roll them over the gravel road between the depot and the general store. Big mail order catalogs were sent to most people in those days; Sears, Montgomery Ward and Spiegel catalogs were ubiquitous. Pretty dresses and shoes, hats, gloves, hosiery were offered as well as heavy duty denim bib overalls, high top work shoes, boots and heavy cotton socks for farmers.

A whole section of the catalogs was devoted to tools which farmers as well as townspeople needed; shovels, axes, crowbars, pitchforks, wire, and twine as well as wheelbarrows, wagons, garden tractors, and high wheel garden cultivators.

My mother was an accomplished seamstress and spent hours looking at all the sewing supplies available. There were cottons, woolens, silks, and linens that could be purchased by the yard; needles, threads, ribbons, bias tape, tape measures and any kind of needle needed as well as lots of different sizes and shapes of scissors. Sewing machines were also offered for sale. Almost anything people needed or wanted was offered in the catalogs and placing orders for merchandise advertised in them was a common practice.

Overnight delivery was not an option and by the time your order arrived at the post office days (or even a week or two) later, you had forgotten what you ordered. It was like Christmas in that respect – packages to open revealing surprises! Catalogs made acquiring needed or wanted supplies convenient and many considered them a lifeline to the outside world. It was interesting and fun to browse through them.

I'd board the train at the depot every Thursday morning during the summer vacation from school and travel to the town where my Aunt Mary lived. As I was a regular passenger on the train, the conductor knew me and would

The Dance in the Kitchen

greet me with a "Good morning, missy. And where are you headed today?"

My aunt had arranged for me to take piano lessons from a lady she knew. The train chugged along clickety clacking over the rails and belched black smoke from its smokestack mounted on the front of the engine right above the cattle catcher grate. I've heard that the cattle catcher grate was a left-over contrivance from the early days of railroading in this country when cattle roamed freely on the prairies. If a cow was accidentally struck by a moving train, the cattle catcher grate would scoot under the cow and the cow had a better chance of surviving. Anyway, that was the story, but I never saw that kind of an incident.

The black smoke billowed alongside the passenger cars and was sucked into the interior where people sat. The windows on either side of the passenger cars were open to try to get some air inside on those hot summer days but there was as much black coal smoke as fresh air, so it didn't help much. When the train went around a curve, the smoke would blow in the other side of the car, so I'd change back and forth often. I tried my best to keep from getting all sooty because I didn't want to get my clean dress dirty.

The train ride to my aunt's town lasted only about 45 minutes and she was usually there waiting to pick me up when the train arrived. I remember only one time when she wasn't there waiting for me. I didn't know what to do so I sat down and waited a while – about thirty minutes. Calling her was not an option because I didn't have access to a telephone.

When she didn't show up, I decided to walk to her house. I knew the way well enough (or so I thought) but things looked different from the passenger seat of her car than they did as a pedestrian. I also had my little suitcase to carry and, as I walked along, it got heavier and heavier. I knew which way to turn when I got to the first corner and felt very pleased with myself, so I picked up my pace a bit. On and on I walked recognizing places and signs as I went along. Other corners had me puzzled. Should I turn right or left? I became confused and, I must admit, a little frightened but as I continued, I saw enough familiar houses or places of business that I recognized, and my confidence returned.

Now, mind you, my aunt's town wasn't large so, if I took a wrong turn, all I had to do was retrace my steps to the end of the block and go the other way. This all took longer but, at last, I knew I was on the right street and picked up my pace to my aunt's front door. She was there when I finally arrived and, because she was worried, she scolded me a little.

"Why didn't you wait for me inside the depot when you got off the train?" and "I've been driving around for the last half hour looking for you. Where were you?"

When she eventually calmed down, we decided she must have driven only the old tried and true way and had missed me when I didn't know for sure which way to turn and went in the wrong direction. We had just missed each other. I was proud of myself for figuring out how to manage by myself and, later that evening, she expressed that she was proud of me too and was glad I was safe. After a bath and a change of clothes, we had a delicious supper on her back porch. Her town had electricity so there were several fans blowing throughout the house and the moving air felt heavenly to me. It made such a relief from the humid, hot summer air.

My grandmother lived with Aunt Mary and, as my aunt worked during the day, grandma was the primary grocery shopper and cook. We went to the neighborhood grocery store every day while I was visiting. She walked but I roller skated. My uncle had given me a pair of roller skates and I kept them at my aunt's house and used them often while there. There were no sidewalks on the farm, and I delighted in roller skating up and down the sidewalk in front of my aunt's house. What joy! Being where there were sidewalks was like a whole new world to me.

The grocery store that my grandmother and I shopped at was two or three blocks away. It was the kind of old-timey store where customers handed their list of items to be purchased to the grocery store owner and he would take those things off the shelves and place them on the counter for customers to approve. There were also aisles of shelves throughout the little store and grandma and I would put things that she needed in a small basket as we went along. I always picked up a can or two of Campbell's Chicken Noodle Soup which was my favorite and I also often threw in a candy bar or two for good measure.

We had to carry everything we purchased back to the house which is the reason grandma went shopping every day. She and I usually had lunch alone, so she'd fix the Campbell's Chicken Noodle Soup and we'd split a candy bar for dessert. Aunt Mary wouldn't have approved so this was our special little secret.

My weekly piano lesson was the next day. The piano teacher's house was two or three blocks away and I walked there. I'd go to the end of the block where Aunt Mary's house was, take a left onto a boulevard and continue until I reached Mrs. Mayberry's house. This was yet another "other world" to me.

The boulevard was covered in short clipped grass and beautiful flowering shrubs as well as taller trees here and there. And, right in the middle, were tall lamp posts topped with electric lights! Each light had a textured, frosted glass shade that dispersed the brightness at night. I was fascinated by all that light and Aunt Mary and I on occasion walked up and down the boulevard after supper at night just so I could enjoy it. We also usually walked around the block back to her house and I was amazed that light was coming from all the windows of the houses all around that block. What a difference electricity made!

My piano lessons went well, and I liked Mrs. Mayberry. I didn't always get a gold star plopped on the top of the music pages, but it was, of course, my own fault when I didn't. Every once in a while I didn't practice as much as I should have.

CHAPTER 22

THRESHING DAY DINNERS

My mother had a degree in Home Economics. She received her college degree at a time in this country when very few women went to college let alone get a degree. My dad's education ended when he finished eighth grade so, they were mismatched as far as learning from books was concerned. They were both intelligent people though, and their learning certainly didn't stop when they no longer attended classes. Dad was a farmer and he needed a "farm wife."

My parents were devoted to one another and mom gladly assumed the role of "farm wife." She brought with her an abundance of skills such as cooking, sewing, and canning as well as common sense. Her cooking and baking skills were excellent and were greatly appreciated on threshing days.

A few times each year men from neighboring farms came to our farm to help dad with harvesting crops. Neighbors helped neighbors harvest as long as it took to get the crop cut and stored. Winter wheat was planted in the fall but not ready for harvest until the middle of summer. It was one of the hottest, dustiest crops to be harvested. Wheat was cut by a machine called a binder that gathered the wheat stalks and was pulled through the field by a team of horses. Another part of the binder gathered the cut wheat together into bundles and tied them with twine. Bundles were next stacked up in what was called shocks and put in windrows to dry until they could be picked up by the men with a pitchfork. Wagon loads of bundles were then carried to the threshing machine in the front of the barn.

The threshing machine was a huge, ungainly machine that separated the wheat from the straw. It reminded me of a brontosaurus because it had a long chute that blew out the chaff the grain left behind. It resembled the long neck of a brontosaurus. The men loaded bundles of wheat into the threshing cylinder and piled up straw that was blown out of the "neck" of the brontosaurus. The pile of straw was half as tall as the barn when it was all finished and was later used for livestock bedding or put on the floor of the chicken house. Chaff blew all around in the air even on only breezy days; It's prickly, fine, and sticks to skin on sweaty hot summer days. This was coupled with insects buzzing around trying their best to get into eyes, ears and noses.

Temperatures were often in the mid 90's during harvest so, all in all, it was a miserable endeavor. But it had to be done!

The whole harvesting effort started very early in the morning when the air was cool, and it also helped the crew to acclimate as the temperatures rose during the day. They worked until mid-morning and then stopped for a break to rest and drink water. I frequently took water to the field for them in a big, stoneware jug that I'd filled with fresh, cool water from the pump by the house. Dad had wrapped layers of burlap around the jug to insulate it and secured it with binder twine which helped it to stay cool. I'd pour water on the burlap which helped keep the water cool then I'd hop on Paddy pony's back. Mom helped me put the jug of water on Paddy's back and we'd slowly walk to the field where the men were resting. Each man drank his fill of cool water from either a tin or a granite-ware cup then stretched out on the ground again for a few more minutes of rest. The ground was cooler than the air so, despite being hot, dirty and prickly, the men went back to work somewhat refreshed. The horses also benefited from resting and were ready to labor on until the next break.

All the while in the kitchen, mom was preparing a huge meal in the steamy hot kitchen for the threshers when they came to the house for their noon meal. She, too, had been up early and, after preparing breakfast for our family, she began the preparations. She had cooked and baked for several days prior to threshing day but much still had to be done. I helped her fry up big platters of chicken, peel, boil and mash potatoes and make gravy. We'd fix beans and squash and cut the homemade bread into slices and put the butter on the table.

She and I picked vegetables from the garden in big, aluminum pans and washed them outside under the pump before taking them into the kitchen to cut up or otherwise prepare for cooking. The scraps we cut off were put in the slop bucket in the kitchen to be fed to the pigs. There were potato peelings, the ends off green beans and carrots, celery leaves, onion peelings, etc. All went into the slop bucket with remnants from the previous day. The bucket was usually dumped in the pig troughs about every third day but, on threshing days, the slop bucket filled more quickly and required emptying more often. That was a task my brother or dad usually did but, on threshing days when there were more scraps, the bucket filled faster, and I was asked to empty it. The pig troughs were right below the elevated platform at the pig pen so I could dump the bucket from that height. I was told not to get in the pen with the pigs because they might knock me down, so I was glad I didn't have to.

Dad butchered both hogs and cattle, so we had both ham and steak. After butchering, the hams were placed in our smokehouse to cure. They had been covered with a salt made especially for that purpose and hung on hooks from the rafters. As I recall, the hams were wrapped in burlap or cotton. A smoky, earthy smell always emanated from the smokehouse while the meat was curing. The smell wafted through the cracks in the building and scented the air all around with the delicious smell of smoked ham. If there's such a thing as a "delicious smell," that was it!

The Dance in the Kitchen

We took our butchered beef to the town where we usually went on Saturday nights to do our weekly grocery shopping. These were the items that my uncle and aunt didn't have available in their general store. Of course, the town had electricity. The town also had a freezer/locker where farmers could bring their butchered meat to be cut up, wrapped, frozen and stored in a rented locker. Mom and I would go to the locker close to the time we left to return home and choose several packages of meat for the coming week. We didn't have a refrigerator at home, so the meat was stored in the basement cool area until needed. I was very nearly scared every time the big, thick, insulated locker door closed behind us, but my mother assured me from time to time that it was safe.

Threshing day dinners (the noon meal was called "dinner") consisted of either fried chicken or a big roast beef or ham steaks. Each meal had all the side dishes one could ever want; mashed potatoes and gravy, green beans, corn, asparagus, carrots, turnips, biscuits or homemade bread. There were large bowls of home-made cottage cheese, cabbage slaw, homemade butter and homemade jelly. We also had squeezed many lemons and made lemonade. Water from the pump was cool and, even though we didn't have ice cubes, the lemonade was very refreshing. The water was too.

As the threshers came in from the field, they put water in a wash pan outside by the pump and washed their hands and faces before coming into the house. It was a cool, refreshing relief which they thoroughly enjoyed, and their talk was animated. When they were finished, they sat on the porch by the kitchen until mom called them inside to eat.

All the men were very polite and thankfully ate their meal in quiet conversation. Nearly all of them had second helpings and, when they were done, mom and I sat down and had our dinner too of what remained in the serving dishes. It was a pleasure to take this break from all the activity in the kitchen during the morning. The threshers could usually be found outside leaning up against a tree resting or taking a nap until it was time to return to the fields for the afternoon harvest. All in all, it was a quiet time of the day and we all appreciated it. When the men returned to the fields, mom and I cleaned up the table and the entire kitchen.

There were often six or eight men helping dad so meal preparation and clean up both took a long time. The dishes were washed in hot sudsy water at the kitchen sink and rinsed in equally hot water. Mom washed and I dried and put the dishes away. Afterwards, mom started thinking and planning food items for supper and I started doing my evening chores.

CHAPTER 23

HOSED DOWN

One of my cousins lived on another farm not too far from us. He was a year older and we liked to play together. We were at his place playing Hide and Seek one day after lunch. My cousin was "it" and I was running around trying to find the best hiding place when I fell into an old outhouse pit! I didn't so much "fall in" as going in feet first. To my horror, I found myself up to my neck in excrement that was still soft enough to sink into. "Help, help, help!!, "I yelled at the top of my lungs. My cousin thought I was trying to fool him and didn't respond right away so I kept yelling, "Help me. I've fallen in a hole!"

He finally did come to my rescue and then we both yelled for his mother to come help us. She was in the house and didn't respond to our calls, so my cousin said, "Grab my hand and I'll pull you out." He tugged and tugged, and I tried to push against the sides of the pit but ended up loosening even more of the contents making it even more slippery. At last, however, we managed to get me up over the edge and he told me to stay there until he came back with his mom.

My aunt was horrified when she saw the predicament I was in and, of course, didn't want to touch me. I smelled to high heaven and was covered in the foul-smelling stuff! She was thankful I wasn't hurt and told me to go up to the house. "Sit down on the ground over there by the hose," she said, and I obeyed. She turned on the hydrant, water ran through the hose and came gushing out the other end. She squirted me off while my cousin went in the house for some rags so I could dry off. I think I had enough waste matter on me to have fertilized their entire vegetable garden!

I sat out in sun while she went inside and telephoned my mom to come get me. "You'd better bring some old towels or rags," she told my mom "so she won't ruin your car seats on the way back home." When my mom saw me, she was equally horrified. "Good thing she hadn't seen me before my aunt had hosed me off," I thought. All the car windows were rolled down on the way home but, even then, it had an unpleasant odor for several days afterwards.

I couldn't take my clothes off at my cousin's house for obvious reasons so, after removing them when we got home, mom filled a big bucket with water from the pump and poured it over me as I sat on the ground. Mom threw all my soiled clothes away and said, "I think you're clean enough now that you can go in the house and take a nice, bath. I'll get the wash tub ready. You get the soap and a washcloth."

The clean bath water was lukewarm and felt so luxurious and relaxing after my traumatic experience that I lingered longer than a bath usually took. The smell of mom's homemade soap was wonderfully clean-smelling, and I created mounds of suds on the washcloth. But, finally, the water became too cool to want to spend more time in, so I emerged all shiny, clean and much sweeter smelling and ready to put on clean clothes. I didn't go outside for the rest of the day and stayed inside reading books and playing the piano. I was even excused from doing my evening chores that day.

My brother, of course, thought it was all hilarious and asked mom if she'd taken a picture of me. I thought he'd never stop razzing me about being "his stinky little sister."

CHAPTER 24

THE SWAMP ROAD

    A few Saturdays during the year when we were leaving home to start the trip to town, my dad would decide that instead of going on the hard surface road, we'd go on the "swamp road." It was surrounded by acres of wet land covered with heavy vegetation of all kinds; huge tropical looking leaves on some trees that were almost black and were glossy. There were chartreuse leaves, yellow leaves, brown leaves – even purple ones. They all overlapped, and vines had tangled some together into big swaying blobs of green. Cattails and other plants thrived in the water and perched on many of them were red winged blackbirds. Turtles poked their heads out of the water as we passed, and we often saw them lined up on a dead log that was half out of the water.

The swamp was home to a variety of frogs too; brown ones, green ones, chartreuse ones and even yellow and orange ones. They were remarkably similar in color to the leaves. It was a beautiful area and, with the windows rolled down on warm weather days, the sounds we heard was a wonderful mixture of birds, bees, insects, frogs all throwing their voices out on the air that blended them together making it sound like a jungle. At least I thought that was surely what a jungle must sound like.

The sights and sounds along the "swamp road" were delightful but I dreaded taking that route to town. It frightened me! It was a narrow dirt road; parts of the sides were eroded, and I was always afraid we'd meet a car coming the other way. Somebody would have to back up and I didn't want it to be us! There was not an inch to spare on either side of the car so backing up was an unrealistic option.

As I remember, the road was about two or three miles long from end to end and there was a narrow, old "bridge" about half-way. There were no sides on the "bridge," and it appeared that someone had only lain hefty planks of timber across a narrow stream. It had been there for years and rattled and wiggled as the car went over it. The nails that held the top planks to the others below were easing their way loose which made me fear the whole thing would collapse and, we'd be plunked in the stream.

Dad knew it scared me, and he always drove very slowly when crossing over the bridge. I wanted it to be over quickly and told him to "go faster, please." He said "It's less dangerous the slower we go" but I was sure he was going slow to heighten my fear.

One time we did meet a car coming the other way and, after getting out of our car and sizing up the situation, dad decided it would be us that had to either back up or somehow turn around.

He said, "I think I have more room to turn around than the other car, so I'll try."

Upon hearing those words, I asked if I could get out and wait until the turning around event was over.

"No. Stay in the car. This won't take very long."

So, I crouched down on the floor of the back seat and hid my eyes. I was terrified! I could hear the car's engine roaring; first in forward gear and then in reverse. With each gear change, I just knew we'd be either plunging head-first into the swamp in front of us or that the rear wheels of the car would slip over the edge of the road and the swamp would claim us that way. First one gear, then the other, going back and forth many times inching our way little by little until we were finally turned completely around and headed back the way we'd come.

"You can get up now," my Dad said.

When I peered out, I saw that we were indeed headed back the way we came. Of course, we lost a lot of time because of these events and ended up taking the hard road to town anyway.

I said something like, "Let's never go to town on the swamp road again, okay?"

CHAPTER 25

OTHER THINGS TO FEAR

It may sound silly, but I suppose everyone is afraid of something; maybe even a few things. Our barn was a couple hundred yards from the house and the ground between the two buildings was covered with hard packed sand from the constant movement of vehicles. There were trees here and there around the edges of the open ground and in the summer, the leaves cast ominous-looking shadows at night. I was often asked in the evening after supper to go to the barn to make sure the doors were all closed and to make sure everything was as it should be before the animals settled down for the night. I hate to admit it, but I was scared to walk from the house to the barn after dark.

The Dance in the Kitchen

The kerosene lantern I carried wasn't very bright and as I waved it back and forth in front of me, the light shone on the leaves and cast creepy looking shadows all around. At times I could hear coyotes or foxes howling in the distance which, of course, added to my dread. I wanted to run as fast as I could but wasn't even to the barn yet let alone having done my chores. The 200-yard trek seemed like a mile and got longer with each step! I mustered my courage and eventually arrived at the barn. Everything was closed, the animals were drowsy, safe, quiet and ready for slumber.

I enjoyed being in the barn at that time of evening even though walking to get there was a challenge. There was the soft sound of the animals breathing and, if hay had just been put in the loft, the air was fragrant with the smell of newly cut alfalfa. Once there I often stayed awhile after doing my chores so I could pick up the new-born kittens and pet and cuddle them. I had done the same thing with the mother cats; they knew me and were not afraid of me. I loved seeing the baby kittens nursing and the contented look on their mother's face. She was all stretched out so each of her kittens could get their share of her milk.

It was such a peaceful, calming scene and I happily lingered. Frequently dad would yell, "Better come back now" which broke my spell and I had to retrace my steps back to the house. The return trip wasn't any less scary, but I always made it without running. I was quite proud of myself for never mentioning my fear to anyone. Maybe it was because I realized my brother would razz me about it if he ever found out. I don't know but my evening chores in the barn after dark never got any easier – until we eventually got electricity and had a tall pole light that lit up the whole area between the house and barn. All I had to do after that was click the switch on in the kitchen.

While it's true that for several weeks after harvest, the alfalfa had a pleasant smell, as it settled and compacted, the odor subsided. Until that time, when the hay was still fresh and softly mounded in the barn loft, I liked to climb the ladder from the ground floor to the loft and swing on the ropes hanging down from the rafters overhead. The ropes were knotted on the ends so all I had to do was place my feet above the knot on either side, grab the rope above with my hands and gradually gain speed and distance so I could let go and fall comfortably into the soft hay underneath.

Sometimes my brother joined me in the fun, but I could tell he thought he was much too old to engage in such folly. I, on the other hand, pursued this pleasure nearly every day until the hay became too compacted to allow much bounce when landing.

One day I'd been enjoying this activity for a while when, to my horror, I saw a huge, black spider just above me. It must have been there all along, but I didn't notice it until it moved on its web. Believe me – it was huge! And black! And wiggly! And looking right at me too! That night at supper, I told my parents about what I'd seen.

"Did you know there are big, black spiders in the barn loft?" I asked.

"How big?" they asked.

"Huge," I said and made a circle with my thumbs and index fingers indicating the hugeness. They looked at each other and then back at me. Unfortunately, my brother was present and called me a "scaredy cat". He never missed a chance to razz me about something and did so for days after.

That ended my rope jumping fun for that harvest season.

CHAPTER 26

TOY AND SPARKY

Besides Oinky, the pig, Paddy pony and the other horses, Rock, Buck and Jack, and the annual supply of new kittens, I had two beautiful dogs as pets. Toy was the first pet dog I remember. She was a Manchester Terrier and was a wiry, little dog. She followed me everywhere and often slept with me at night. She'd often accompany me on my forays around the farm and I regarded her as a close friend. We loved each other.

Dad came to the house one day and said he'd found Toy out by the hedgerow by the horse lot and she dead.

"What happened?!," I asked in disbelief.

"Looks like a fox killed her." He said. "Her throat was slit."

I cried for days.

The Dance in the Kitchen

A couple of weeks after school started that fall, I came home to find a beautiful black and white Border Collie. He was just a puppy and dad had purchased him from a neighbor whose female dog had given birth to several puppies. His eyes sparkled so we named him Sparky. He was a bigger dog than Toy and had a different disposition, but he and I became fast friends too. He also followed me everywhere I went until he, too, had covered every one of the 280 acres.

Sparky and I liked to pack a picnic lunch in the morning and head out to an area of the farm that I called "the desert." It was about 20 acres of sand hills with desert-like vegetation growing sparsely on it. Dad said it wouldn't grow any useful crop, so he left it to mother nature. As the sand was blown by the wind, it mounded up here and there creating undulations and small dunes. It was a great place to play and pretend Sparky and I were Egyptians.

When we got hungry, I'd unpack our picnic of sandwiches and Kool Aid. Sparky, of course, had water with his sandwich. On real hot summer days, we would walk on to Quiver Creek to cool off. On those days Quiver Creek became the Nile River to me. He loved being in the water as much as I did and by the time we got home again, we were both dry.

Unlike Toy, Sparky slept on the floor beside my bed and I found great comfort in hearing him breathe and moan in his sleep. He was a wonderful companion.

CHAPTER 27

HEDGE ROWS

There were old, time-worn hedgerows separating many fields on the farm. They were trees planted in earlier times whose inedible fruit is green and about the size of a softball. As they grew and became overlapping and intertwined, the trees served as a fence to protect livestock from wandering away. The hedgerows formed a boundary that was nearly impenetrable to livestock, but it had to be maintained regularly. They were already quite ancient when I was a child and my dad and brother kept constant vigilance and repaired any breaches when necessary.

Sometimes some of the young, supple branches could be tied to adjacent stronger, more mature branches to encourage them to grow where they would fill the breach but, other times, it was necessary to dig post holes and cover the opening with fence material. Over time, as the trees grew older, the new growth was meager, and more and more openings appeared that had to be filled. As a result, my dad and brother spent more hours (and often entire days) mending gaps in the hedgerows.

The fence posts were cut from timber on our property, sawed into shorter lengths and loaded on a wagon pulled by a team of horses; usually Rock and Buck because they were the most reliable team. When enough had been cut for the task at hand, the posts were hauled to the site to be repaired, off-loaded and ready to be placed in the ground. Of course, holes had to be dug to put each post in and that was done by hand. Dad always seemed to know exactly how every task was done and putting up fencing was no exception. He used a post hole digger which was a kind of double-sided shovel with a long handle. It worked best when the ground was wet or, at least, moist so as the shovel was plunged into the ground, it started to dig down. I can remember my dad raising his arms up over his head while holding the shovel handle and then plunging it down into the soft ground repeatedly until the hole was deep enough to support the post. My brother wasn't as tall as my dad, so it took him longer to dig a hole of sufficient depth. It was exhausting work!

The post holes had to dry out for a day or two before the posts could be lowered into position. Then the hole was filled with dirt and packed down using a tamping tool which forced the dirt down into the hole by a repeated stroke. More dirt was piled up around the base of the post and tamped down by their shoes. Rain would sometimes drop the soil level around the post and, when that happened, more dirt had to be piled up and tamped down into the hole later.

Barbed wire came in big rolls and had to be unrolled and cut to length with a special wire cutter so it could be attached to the fence posts with big, sturdy wire staples. This was a two-man job and wearing leather gloves was a requirement. The wire had to be pulled taut so it wouldn't sag. Dad would loop a bit of the wire around a steel rod, twist, and pull as hard as he could until it was straight. My brother would then staple the wire in place on the post. They took turns doing this as pulling was the hardest job.

Not all the fence posts were straight, but it didn't matter because they were part of the hedgerow and, after a while, were camouflaged by the branches and leaves and were nearly invisible.

Paddy and I would occasionally ride out to where they were digging with water and sandwiches; at other times it was cake or pie fresh from the oven. That gave them a chance to take a break and rest in the shade but, as I remember, putting up new fences was usually done in the fall or early winter after the crops had been harvested.

CHAPTER. 28

CHURCH ON SUNDAY

We went to church every Sunday morning; mom, dad, my brother and me. We'd all had our baths on Saturday evening, and it was a joy to get all dressed up on Sunday mornings. Being "all dressed up" meant that we wore clothes that were held in reserve for going to church or to wear for special occasions. Women and girls wore pretty hats and gloves and men and boys wore suits, white shirts and neckties. All the women and girls wore dresses or skirts and blouses; not a one wore what was called "slacks" back then.

Most of the people in the congregation were farmers and there was quite a difference between how they looked on Sunday mornings compared to how they looked when at home working in the fields or tending to chores around the barn and house.

My aunts Mary and Evangeline had given me a white, fur muff and wrap-around hat that tied under my chin and I delighted in wearing them to church on cold, winter days. It was fun to sit with a friend and her family or my family during the church service. My friends and I found lots of occasions to giggle and our respective mothers would crossly look at us and say, "Hush!" That only increased our urge to giggle, however, and sometimes we even had to be split up during the service. That meant that a parent was sitting between us which prompted us to lean forward a bit and make faces at each other causing us to giggle again.

It was always such a relief when the service was over, and we could go outside again. This was our chance to get together with more friends. As young children, we ran around the church grounds chasing each other and, as young adults, the girls and boys tended to be in separate groups.

Of course, the girls talked about the boys and discussed and giggled about who was the cutest and, the boys obviously cast glancing eyes in the direction of the girls and probably took turns saying who they thought was the prettiest. We were all at an age where the two sexes seldom mingled but there was a lot of conjecturing about what would happen when they did.

Sunday was just about the only day when mom didn't have to worry about preparing food for our family. There were a couple of restaurants in our little town and, after saying good-bye to our friends at church, we'd drive to one of them. Restaurants weren't fancy in small, farm towns, but it was a real treat to look at all the choices on the menu, tell a waitress what you wanted and just sit and wait until the food was brought to the table. When we ate at home, everyone ate the same thing but at a restaurant, we could all get something different.

CHAPTER 29

HOMEMADE ICE CREAM AND WATERMELON

We changed into more comfortable clothes when we got back home, and we all did only those chores that absolutely had to be done. I checked to make sure the chickens had enough water, dad milked the cows, my brother forked hay into the animals' mangers and mom made plans for a light supper. We often had grilled cheese sandwiches and homemade tomato soup on these occasions, but now and then it was followed by a very special (and rare) dessert like homemade ice cream or cold watermelon.

It was not an easy task to make homemade ice cream. It involved getting ice in chunks from either my uncle and aunt's store or from the freezer/locker in town. Either way, it had to be wrapped in several layers of burlap, surrounded by straw and wrapped in burlap again. If we got the ice from either source and, if it was wrapped in this manner, there would be enough left despite the summer heat so that when Sunday afternoon came, it could be crushed and packed around a metal cylinder inside our manual ice cream freezer. Inside the cylinder were the delicious liquid ingredients that mom had stirred together; fresh cream, egg yolks, vanilla and sugar. Mom had made the mixture to be frozen in the morning before we left for church and it had been in the cool room in the basement all day.

When we were ready to begin freezing the mixture, the ice was put in a canvas bag and crushed with a heavy mallet that was the same one mom used for tenderizing meat. The crushed ice was packed around the cylinder slightly above the level of the mixture in the middle of the can and sprinkled with coarse rock salt. The ice had to be packed down solidly with a wooden spoon and left to stand for five minutes before starting to turn the crank.

Dad, my brother and I took turns rotating the crank. Mom sat that activity out. When the ice cream was frozen, the crank turned with difficulty until it was nearly impossible to turn it at all. We all had our dishes ready to receive the frozen contents and usually dipped a large long-handled spoon or an ice cream scoop into the frozen yumminess. Mom often made chocolate sauce to be drizzled over the top for added enjoyment. Sometimes we'd sprinkle peanuts or chopped walnuts on top of the chocolate.

Watermelon, of course, was a much easier dessert. We had watermelons of our own planted in a big field not far from the house and, when they were ripe, one of my chores was to pull my wagon to that field and bring back as many as I could. No one cared so much if the watermelons were cold (or even cool) but, occasionally, mom would put one in the basement cool room to be enjoyed later in the day. Compared to making ice cream, that was a snap and enjoyed just as much.

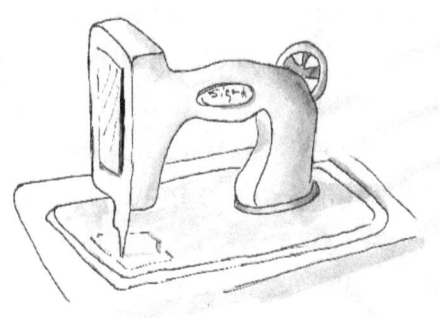

CHAPTER 30

MOM'S SEWING SKILLS

Mom thought it was important to teach me how to sew and cook. Remember – she was a college graduate with a degree in Home Economics. I wasn't very interested in either pursuit, but she persisted, and I did manage to learn a little about both. They might be called "survival skills" today. There was plenty to help with both in preparing the daily meals for just our family as well as on special days when threshers or other occasional helpers were in the kitchen for noon meals.

I would often bring fresh vegetables in from the garden and would also be asked to "clean" them. This involved snipping the ends off green beans and breaking them in the middle. That made a snapping sound and green beans were often called "snap" beans. If I chose to pull carrots from the ground, the tops had to be cut off (these went in the pig slop bucket), they had to be scraped and cut into smaller pieces ready to be put in water and boiled until they were soft enough to eat. A lot of slicing, dicing and chopping noises could be heard coming from the kitchen when meals were being prepared. Pounding noises were also heard on those days when mom used a meat mallet to flatten chicken, beef or pork for certain delicious recipes calling for thinner pieces of meat. Cube steaks and pork cutlets come to mind. Pounding with the toothed side of the mallet tenderized the meat making it easier to eat. I often peeled potatoes, cooked them and mashed them when they were soft enough. You can imagine how good they tasted using homemade butter and fresh milk.

Mom's pies were outstanding! She could make any kind of pie and we all had our favorites. Mine was chocolate, dad's favorite was rhubarb, and my brother's favorite was apple. It's strange that I don't remember what mom's favorite was. We all savored every bite of every kind she made and many times she made two or three different kinds a day. She wanted a variety on those days when men who had helped dad in the fields were going to be at the table. Mom became known as the local "best pie baker" which, of course, made her feel modestly proud.

She almost always made an angel food cake "from scratch" on our respective birthdays. That required 12 egg whites from eggs which I was asked to gather from the chicken house. In the meantime, mom had gathered all the ingredients and tools necessary to make this treat. It was time-consuming hard work without electricity. She had to beat the egg whites in a large bowl with a wire whip until they were foamy, gradually add small amounts of sugar at a time and continue beating until the meringue held stiff peaks. Flavoring was added and a mixture of flour and sugar was sifted by hand over the meringue and, finally, folded into it. All this batter was pushed into a tube pan and baked in the oven of the old cook stove.

When done, it was inverted on a bottle or funnel and left to hang until it was cold. When it was turned right side up again on a pretty plate, she made creamy icing; sometimes white but the icing on my cake was always pink. She used juice from a jar of maraschino cherries instead of water. The cherries were saved and, at serving time, she placed one or two cherries on each slice for added goodness and beauty. My birthday was in May and we frequently made homemade ice cream to go with the cake. All the other family birthdays were in the fall or winter and, ice cream wasn't as much a treat in cold weather.

My sewing attempts were dismal.

We had a treadle style Singer sewing machine and mom suggested I practice operating the treadle with my feet for a few minutes every practice session. The needle had been removed and there was no cloth so all I had to do was push back and forth with my feet on the treadle to create a consistent rhythm; back and forth, back and forth. After a few days of doing that, I went on to the next step. Mom put a piece of cloth under the presser foot and showed me how to lower it. Next I had to operate the treadle while keeping an eye on the cloth.

I did okay with that step and one day she said, "I think you're ready for me to put the needle in now" and she inserted it in its holder. Now there were three things to think about – and all at once; push back and forth on the treadle, place the cloth under the presser foot and watch the needle going up and down with each push on the treadle. It seemed a lot more intimidating with the sharp needle shining menacingly as it went up and down. The trick was to hold the cloth in place with my left hand, so it moved in a straight-line while being pushed forward by the machine. The needle hadn't been threaded at this point because my mother was trying to acquaint me with only one thing at a time. I still wasn't really "sewing" but that was the next step.

When she thought I'd satisfactorily accomplished those three steps, she showed me how to thread the needle. That was simple, and I felt my confidence building. I placed my feet on the treadle, put the cloth in position under the presser foot, lowered it, and with trepidation slowly pushed back and forth on the treadle. The needle continued moving up and down and, after a short time, was moving rhythmically leaving behind a nice, straight row of stitches in the cloth.

I thought it was fun and decided to make the needle go up and down faster. That turned out to be a big mistake! Suddenly, I got all the steps mixed up and instead of being able to slow down (for whatever reason), my feet pushed harder and faster on the treadle. In the confusion of everything happening at once; treadle moving rapidly and seemingly out of control, gleaming needle blurred by the speed and cloth nearly at the end, all of a sudden, the needle had pierced my right thumb through the nail and I was held fast.

I screamed, "Mom!'

She was in the kitchen in the next room and came running to see what was wrong. There I was, unable to move, with blood all over the top of the sewing machine.

She extracted the needle from my thumb and pulled my whole arm up over my head. In the meantime, my brother, hearing my yell, came downstairs to see what the commotion was about and, when he saw my bloody hand, promptly passed out. So, there he was unconscious on the floor and there I was with my arm up over my head with blood running down it. And there was my mom trying to tend to both of us going back and forth, back and forth. She wrapped my thumb in a damp, clean cloth and said,

"Keep your arm up until I see about your brother."

Then she went to him with another damp, clean cloth, dabbed it on his forehead and gently patted him on the cheeks attempting to wake him up. It seemed ages passed until she got back to me. My thumb was painful, and I was bawling like a baby.

"Some courageous big brother," I thought, "What a sissy!"

No one knew until then that he went weak in the knees at the sight of blood. I, of course, chided him about that for years afterwards threatening to tell his friends that he was a sissy and passed out at the mere sight of blood.

"If you don't leave me alone, I'll tell your friends what a sissy you are!"

It worked for a while but, eventually, my threat lost its effect and I couldn't think of anything new to threaten him with. Basically, we got along quite well considering we were brother and sister and our age difference but, there were times I loathed him.

I gave up trying to learn how to sew for a long time after that incident. I think it was my mother who decided I was still too young to attempt it. I wasn't at all sorry. I didn't care for it anyway. I would much rather be outside riding Paddy or roaming around the farm looking for new places to play.

CHAPTER 31

ELECTRICITY AT LAST!

It was as if a miracle had happened; there was light everywhere!

We could flip a switch and light shone when and where we wanted. No more kerosene lamps in the house, no more kerosene lanterns or flashlights for outdoor chores after dark; all we had to do now was flip a switch. We could now warm the brooder house for the baby chicks by leaving a low wattage electric bulb on during the night and not have to worry about a kerosene heater tipping over and starting a fire. I could go to the barn after dark to do my evening chores by turning on the pole light.

There were still shadows that moved threateningly and I still had trepidations about traversing the space between the house and barn, but the light helped a lot. It extended the light more evenly over the entire area and I could see over a much broader expanse of ground. When I got to the barn, all I had to do was open the door and turn on the switch to light up the interior. The livestock never gave any indication that they noticed. The cows continued to chew their cuds and the horses kept eating hay out of their manger.

I was thrilled with the convenience of electricity and thought it odd the animals didn't notice at all. The baby kittens and their mother continued to have their nest in the cow's manger; their behavior didn't change either.

Our behavior changed, however. We were all positively giddy for a couple of weeks after the R.E.A. crew had installed the tall poles and electric wires necessary to transmit the current to various properties in our area. We now had poles and wires alongside our lane leading out to the public dirt road. Other tall poles dotted our place around the house and barn. We were amazed by what a difference electricity made. It transformed our lives.

Way back in 1936, congress passed the R.E.A. (Rural Electrification Act). Electricity was commonplace in cities and even towns, but it was unavailable on farms and ranches. Prior to that time, it was thought that providing rural America with electricity was not economically possible. In 1935 President Franklin Roosevelt issued an Executive Order that got the ball rolling and, within a few years, the rural areas of America began to light up.

The federal government sent out crews of R.E.A. workers to install power lines which enabled America's countryside to have electricity in their houses as well as barns and other out-buildings. This consisted mostly of a ceiling-mounted light fixture in each room that was controlled by a single switch near a door. I remember we had several overhead lights in the barn. It was much larger than the house, of course, and required more fixtures. There were two light fixtures in the kitchen too because it was the largest, if not the busiest, room in the house but all the other rooms, both upstairs and down, had only one fixture dangling in the middle of the ceiling.

Unless you were sitting right under it, it was still difficult to see, but it was a definite improvement over kerosene lamps! Each room in the house had one outlet. The barn had several outlets and were distributed throughout both in the hayloft and the stalls of the horses and cows. The stalls also had bare electric light bulbs dangling from the ends of long black cords that swayed, creating strange light patterns when the wind blew through.

When there was a breeze, and it moved the long, black cords, the light moved too; swaying back and forth, back and forth. It was frustrating to keep track of what you were doing as it seemed to make otherwise stationary objects bounce around. It made me wobbly and I sometimes tried to make the bulb stay still by reaching up and steadying it with my pitchfork. It continued to sway, of course, as long as there was a draft through the barn.

When the evening chores in the barn were done, all I had to do was flip the light switch off and head back to the house. As time went on, I began to walk slower on the return trip and began to notice other things that I'd overlooked before because of my unrealistic fear of the dark before we had electricity. The pole light illuminated a wide swath, but it was concentrated. If I stepped outside that circle of light and looked up, I could see millions of stars that dotted the sky.

I discovered when the moon was full, I didn't need the pole light at all and began to take pleasure in dawdling on my way back to the house. "What took you so long?" someone at the house would ask when I returned. Strangely, the ability to step back into the circle of light from the pole light increased my self-confidence but, I was getting older which may have had something to do with it. Anyway, I was no longer the "scaredy cat" that my brother said I was. I enjoyed being outside on my own both day and night.

We still didn't have air conditioning, of course. The only place to cool off was in a movie theater. The advertisements for theaters said, "air cooled" and stepping off the street into the theater was like stepping from the middle of hot summer into cool, fall air. Every once in a while the whole family would go to a movie on Saturday afternoons before shopping just to relax and cool off. We did not, however, have air conditioning on the farm.

I don't remember that any of our farm neighbors had air conditioners either. Even my uncle and aunt at the general store didn't have air conditioning even though they'd had electricity for a few years. I can remember the big, black fans overhead throwing out hot air in their store and post office.

The Dance in the Kitchen

One of the first things mom and dad did after electricity came to our farm was to buy several fans; not one for every room, however. There were two in the kitchen; one oscillating and one that directed the air in only one position. I had the privilege of taking the "one position" fan to my bedroom at night and I'd set it to blow directly on me as I slept. It helped a lot and made sleeping without sweating possible especially when I set the fan in an open window; it sucked in cooler air from outside. There were other fans downstairs too but, at bedtime, everyone would take one of them upstairs to help them sleep. Such a relief!

Everyone slept better.

CHAPTER 32

FREEZER, RADIO, REFRIGERATOR

The very first electrical convenience my parents purchased was a chest type food freezer. It was enormous and stood gleaming white in the kitchen. Mom laid a long rag rug that she'd made on the top to protect the smooth, shiny surface. It clicked on and hummed quietly until it shut off at the end of its cycle. It was a source of many remarks made while we were eating at the nearby table. "Listen, it's on now" or "I think I just heard it click off" or "How long before it comes on again do you think?"

Mom was just happy that she didn't have to worry about getting meat from the locker/freezer in town anymore and would eventually have all the meat that my dad butchered right there in that freezer in her very own kitchen. For her it meant she could take something out of the freezer

The Dance in the Kitchen

in the morning to thaw and fix it later in the same day. It saved her a lot of time.

Dad's first purchase after we had electricity was a radio. He justified its purchase by saying he wanted to be able to listen to the evening news and the weather forecasts. He didn't have to justify it, of course, but I guess it just made him feel better. He certainly didn't want anyone to think he was frivolous!

The radio was a big, brown wooden upright box on turned legs; probably walnut. It was a beautiful piece of furniture that brought the outside world into our home. It had a tiny, little dial in the middle towards the top that lit up so you could see the stations pass when the knob was turned. With each passing station, the radio hissed, grated or screeched until it finally stopped at a station number that could be heard clearly. The radio was in the dining room, but we all re-arranged our chairs to hover around this electric brown marvel and listen to voices from afar bringing us the news or singing or stories.

It was a marvel!

My brother and I hurried home from school as fast as we could and did our chores quickly so we could listen to the serial stories; The Lone Ranger, Red Ryder. Others were The Phantom, Roy Rogers and Dale Evans. Gene Autry was called "The Singing Cowboy" but Roy Rogers and Dale Evans always sang "Happy Trails to You" at the end of their broadcast. I can still hum that. My brother and I both enjoyed Buck Rogers, Flash Gordon, Yukon King, The

Cisco Kid and Terry and the Pirates. He liked Dick Tracy, but it was not my favorite, so I didn't listen to that.

After supper, dad and mom listened intently to "Gabriel Heater and the News" or "Walter Winchell" which I found boring. After all, what did what was happening in Germany or Japan have anything to do with me?! It wasn't long before there was a smaller radio in the kitchen too, so mom could listen to "Arthur Godfrey and Friends" while preparing food. I can still hear the Irish tenor, Dennis Day singing "My Wild Irish Rose" and "When Irish Eyes Are Smiling." She also liked to listen to "The Art Linkletter Show" which was one of her favorites. When she wasn't listening to a talk show on the radio, she'd turn the dial to a music station that played many of the same tunes she played on the piano.

She was listening to the news one day on the kitchen radio when she quickly turned up the volume and started excitedly jumping around in circles.

"Go out to the field where your dad's plowing," she said, "and tell him the war's over!"

I ran as fast as I could until I saw dad on the tractor and waved for him to stop. "Mom said to tell you the war's over," I said.

"What?" he said.

"The war's over!" I repeated.

We ran together as fast as our legs would carry us back to the house. Mom was waiting at the kitchen door. Dad grabbed her and together they danced joyfully all around the kitchen whooping and laughing. It was a wonderful sight for me to see my parents having such a happy moment and I've never forgotten their joy.

Looking back, it seems strange that we didn't get a refrigerator right away, but I think it was because the "cool room" in the basement still served its purpose. The freezer was considered more important because the meat that was butchered on the farm could be more quickly frozen. It also represented a savings too as they didn't have to rent freezer/locker space in town anymore.

We did finally have a refrigerator in the kitchen too and things like milk, homemade butter or cottage cheese kept much longer. We still chilled watermelons in a big galvanized tub of cool water outside but, if there was any left, it went in the refrigerator.

CHAPTER 33

INDOOR PLUMBING

Indoor plumbing was as miraculous to us as electricity and we eventually had pipes installed that brought water inside just by turning on faucets. There was a hydrant outside near the pump and now all I had to do was turn it on and fill buckets with water to take to the chickens; a lot easier than priming the pump and working the handle up and down. The windmill was still the main provider of water for the horse tank; not much had changed around the barn lots.

The biggest change occurred when dad and my brother converted a storage room on the first floor into an indoor bathroom. This was another miracle! Now we had a bathtub and a sink and didn't have to use the outhouse anymore. We could put a plug in the drain of the bathtub and fill it with water just by turning on the faucet. Mom no longer had to keep water hot on the stove for all our baths because we now had hot and cold running water and it was available all the time. We could also all enjoy bathing in clean water.

The old wash house was now obsolete. Mom and dad purchased an electric washing machine and put it in the basement under the kitchen. Mom no longer had to make a roaring fire in the old cookstove; hot water was available now just by turning on the tap, and the new wringer/washer could be plugged into electricity! The galvanized wash tubs still stood alongside to rinse the sudsy clothes but, each had a drain hose in the bottom so the tubs could be emptied into the floor drain. Each tub could be emptied and refilled as often as needed.

From then on, the washing machine did most of the work on laundry day, but mom still had to scrub some of dad's dirtiest overalls on the washboard before putting them in the washing machine. Everything that was formerly soiled was perfectly clean before it was hung on the clothesline. There is no artificial scent that's as pleasant as clothes hung on an outdoors clothesline.

It's the cleanest, freshest smell in the world!

JANE SELLIER

AFTER WORD

When I was a child, I used to dream that someday there would be a machine that washed dishes. Of course, you must remember that I grew up on a farm where we didn't have running water or electricity. It still seems miraculous to me that now I can just push a button or two on my dishwasher and after a bit of water sloshing around and a little heat, my dishes are shiny and clean and ready to be put back in the cabinets.

I think my washing machine is a miracle too. And television. And air conditioning. Even my lawnmower is a miracle. All I have to do is recharge the battery by plugging it into an electric outlet, push a button to start it and away I go!

I grew up on a farm in central Illinois and rode my pony down dusty lanes. I wandered through rows of corn taller than I was on hot summer days. Sometimes at night, I'd go out at dusk and lay between the rows of tall corn because the ground felt cool and I liked to listen to the sounds the corn made as it grew taller.

I'm grateful I had excellent teachers when I started school in the one room country schoolhouse I attended. I went on later to be a teacher myself and used those former teachers of mine as role models.

My family sold the farm and we moved to a small town on the Illinois River when I was a Sophomore in high school. I started dating and we'd go to football games, dances and other school events together. In the summer, my friends and I would go swimming in the Illinois River and lay on the beach soaking up the sun. I learned to water ski on that river too.

There was a city pool not far from where I lived and I'd meet my friends there to cool off on hot, summer days. I went on dates at night and joined friends for slumber parties. There was ice skating in the winter on a pond and bonfires in the cold, open air. We roasted hot dogs and marshmallows and warmed our hands by the fire.

At the time I didn't realize how amazing my parents were or how they went about their everyday affairs would influence me. Mom could do anything; she sewed, upholstered furniture, wallpapered and kept the accounts for the farm business. In addition, she cooked delicious meals, washed dishes and clothes. She butchered chickens and made butter and soap.

Dad was a hard worker and knew what and when to plant crops. If a machine that he needed broke down, he was able to fix it. There were times, however, that he needed the skills of the local blacksmith.

The blacksmith shop in Topeka, Illinois was across the street and down a little way from my aunt and uncle's general store. It was sooty black inside and out and I liked to go there with my dad. There were big, wide double doors on the front that opened like barn doors which the blacksmith propped open with a board. Everything was the same charcoal black color – even the man and his leather apron. Everyone liked my dad, so the blacksmith was always glad to see him. They'd talk and joke together for a while which gave me the chance to investigate the inside of the building.

A big, square stone and brick platform held glowing embers that the blacksmith would thrust metal into to heat so he could pound it into the desired shape on his anvil. Several buckets of water sat at the base of the anvil and were used for quenching the metal. I was fascinated by the sound and the hissing puff of steam that rose up as the hot metal hit the water. The walls of the building were lined with the tools of his trade; hammers, tongs, trammels, crowbars that were all hanging on hand wrought black, square nails. There were also ropes and pullies, wooden work benches, a heap of coal, a pile of wood and a huge roll top desk with a closed tambour top. It was rolled open only when dad paid for the services. I was amazed at how clean it was inside. The blacksmith's fingerprints always smudged the receipt, and, for some reason, that reminded me of detective stories we listened to on the radio; programs like Dick Tracy and Sam Spade.

Dad also cut down trees and planted others. He plowed, raked and harrowed. I remember when he would pick a bouquet of wildflowers for my mom and put his arms around her when he gave them to her. He read stories to me and played ball with my brother.

My parents loved each other and were committed to their marriage and children. Together they survived the grief of losing their first-born son. They were admirable people. I'm glad I was one of their children.

My childhood on a farm was not uncommon, but it's a way of life that has become more uncommon over the years.

I'll be forever grateful that I was able to experience all that farm life offered me as a child growing up.

THE END

www.ingramcontent.com/pod-product-compliance
Lightning Source LLC
Chambersburg PA
CBHW032106280426
43661CB00110B/1390/J